Monty's Surprise

First published in 2008
by Wayland

Text copyright © Karen Wallace 2008
Illustration copyright © Lisa Williams 2008

Wayland
338 Euston Road
London NW1 3BH

Wayland Australia
Hachette Children's Books
Level 17/207 Kent Street
Sydney, NSW 2000

The rights of Karen Wallace to be identified as the Author and
Lisa Williams to be identified as the Illustrator of this Work have been
asserted by them in accordance with the Copyright, Designs and Patents Act, 1988.

Series Editor: Louise John
Cover design: Paul Cherrill
Design: D.R.ink
Consultant: Shirley Bickler

A CIP catalogue record for this book is available from the British Library.

ISBN 9780750254014

Printed in China

Wayland is a division of Hachette Children's Books,
an Hachette Livre UK Company
www.hachettelivre.co.uk

Monty's Surprise

Written by Karen Wallace
Illustrated by Lisa Williams

WAYLAND

It was breakfast time in the jungle and Monty the Monkey was cross.

He pushed away his bowl of green leaves.

"Why are you cross?" asked Flora the Elephant.

Monty said nothing and
stuck out his tongue.

"Please, tell us," said Spots the Leopard.

8

But Monty turned his back.

Lulu the Parrot landed on a branch nearby.

"I think you're just hungry," she said. "Eat up your green leaves and you'll feel better."

"I don't want green leaves!"
shouted Monty. "I'm not
eating them!"

Flora pulled out a small tree from the ground.

"Try some twigs. They're very tasty," she said.

"I don't want twigs,"
said Monty.

He stomped away feeling very cross.

"What shall we do?"
asked Spots.

"We must find out what
Monty wants for his breakfast,"
said Lulu.

Monty's friends found him sitting under a big tree.

"Try these beetles," said Lulu.
"I found them for you."

19

"Or how about a delicious snake?" asked Spots. "Snakes are my favourite food."

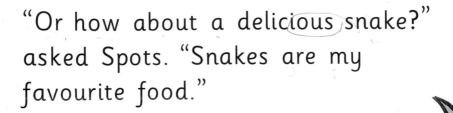

"I don't want a snake or beetles!" said Monty.

"So, what DO you want for breakfast?" asked all his friends together.

"I don't KNOW!" shouted Monty, and he wanted to cry because he was very hungry.

Suddenly a strong wind shook the branches in the tree above Monty's head.

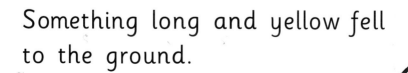

Something long and yellow fell
to the ground.

25

"What's that?" asked Flora.
"It's a banana, of course,"
said Monty.

Monty picked up the banana.

He peeled back the skin and
took a big bite.

"What do you think?" asked Spots
the Leopard.

Monty's friends held their breath.

"I think I want bananas for breakfast!" cried Monty, and a big smile spread over his face.

START READING is a series of highly enjoyable books for beginner readers. They have been carefully graded to match the Book Bands widely used in schools. This enables readers to be sure they choose books that match their own reading ability.

The Bands are:

Pink / Band 1
Red / Band 2
Yellow / Band 3
Blue / Band 4
Green / Band 5
Orange / Band 6
Turquoise / Band 7
Purple / Band 8
Gold / Band 9

START READING books can be read independently or shared with an adult. They promote the enjoyment of reading through satisfying stories supported by fun illustrations.

Karen Wallace was brought up in a log cabin in Canada. She has written lots of different books for children, fiction and non-fiction, and even won a few awards. Karen likes writing funny books because she can laugh at her own jokes! She has two sons and two cats. The sons have grown up and left home but the cats are still around.

Lisa Williams did her first drawing at 15 months old – it was a worm! She told her mum to write 'Worm' underneath the picture. When she was five, she decided that she wanted to be an illustrator when she grew up. She has always loved drawing animals and hopes that you will enjoy this book...